I am wł
put together, I am put
together. I might not have
myself figured out, but I
have my materials and
financials figured out...
you can see it by the car I
drive, the condition of my
hair and skin, and by the
brands I wear. From my
sunglasses to my shoes,
and everything in between
I look like you want to be

me, or at least I make you a little insecure about something. Because I, I have a balanced ego, I'm proud of myself and I show it with all these... things.

What happens when we start to feed our ego externally rather than our health and soul internally? Of course, there is a middle ground, I call it my median in action (MIA). Which, we will touch on later. But, how do we keep aware of if we are feeding our ego, which lead to unexpected stresses and feeling of disconnectedness or are we feeding our internal inspiration leaving us feel more connected and growing into our

community. And how do
we know the difference?

Chapter 1

Perception of success

Who is more successful the one with the sport car, full hair, great skin, world traveler with that skin glow or the one who is a nature center volunteer, expressive poetically and artfully, who takes the time to stop and understand?

Or are they the same person?

So, we can have health, luxuries, explored passions, hair appointments, and be a life learner with the sport car who happens to volunteer where our hearts feel is needed. Do not judge a book by its cover, right?

So where does this idea that Success is not sexually transmitted come from? It comes from the idea any act we do is either internally motivated from our passions beliefs or inspirations or externally learned called upon by what we think we are supposed to be like, look like, or act like. Success is not sexually transmitted, we are either looking for a way to look how we think we are supposed to based on external factors or we are internally growing into our passions and inspirations. One is an act from fear the other is an act out of love. Fear being if we don't look, act or own a certain thing or a way that we want to measure up to what we feel we need to. Love being if we grow our passions, we are so inspired by that we want to share with others our love for this look, act or way of living.

Thus MIA came to use, Median In Action, the break down of this is between the pieces of me that feed my internal passions and internal growths with the pieces of me that feed into how I think something will make me appear. MIA (Median In Action) is the meeting of internal passion, internal growth for my curiosity and my external drive for what I desire.

The phrase "success is not sexually transmitted" is the

idea if we are not aware of where our motives for how we live we will pursue a life to look as though we are ok.. good... better than the next. Finding a mate for life is one of the largest components to human nature. All things we are motivated by comes out in our decisions, then into our lives, then into what we are attracted to and what is attracted to us.

If my main motive from the start is to have money, the sport car, and to have pictures of all the trip so others can see how lavish my life looks, I will most likely continue to feed external factors. I will most likely be attracting others who are drawn to these

external factors... not me.
If my main motive is to find
my passion grow it and
share it, to give back to my
community and to grow the
love I have for my
inspirations and the areas
of life I find alluring, I will
most likely attract those
who see my acts and my
acts from my passion, I will
most likely attract others
who also have the same

cares for the environment and are interested in me and the same engagements I am curious about.

Leading into finding a life partner, soul mate, wife, husband, other half, whatever you call it that is a fulfilling relationship.

What we want, what we are, and what we need:

-What we think we want vs what we find fulfilling.

-What we put out there that we are, vs what we truly are.

-what we think we need compared to what we actually need.

These are aspects of your life only you know, and

only you can and will uncover.

For example, I thought I wanted to have every basic Prada purse, with a cleaner and a cook and a driver, I thought I wanted to be able to pay for my friends to come visit me... where ever I was in the world.

What I really wanted was to not have to carry

anything, and Prada didn't make me happier. I really wanted friends who knew me truly.

I thought I needed the largest walk in closet with a jacuzzi and marble floors and a massage every other day and if I were to have just been this skinny, I wouldn't need anything.

I found after breaking it down for myself that I really only NEED air, to nourish my body with, good food, hydration, meditation and to grow my passions.

The closet became a mess, the jacuzzi went nearly unused, and starving myself left me so miserable.

So then what is the
breakdown of my definition
of 'success'? what does
success mean to me as an
individual? Nearly nothing.
Success or fail. In my
experience, the breakdown
of succeeding is this; a
lead to continued learning,
while also knowing that in
this instant this worked to
continue to the next level
of learning, which may not

work again and most likely will not be the same exact variables again. So ultimately for me success is just reaching the next level or phase of learning not one better than the other only broadening my experience and awareness within one area or study or practice. Failing, means continued learning. 'Failing' has proven to show me many times that, whatever instant I was considering a 'fail' lead me to a more enjoyable and rewarding experience to learn in. Ultimately the idea of success or fail pertaining to specific events, trails, and or instances have been proven to hold a better experience when viewing the situation as a learning

one rather than a pass/fail
or success/regress.

Chapter 2

How 'success' in not sexually transmitted.

Marry for love, look for internal connection, seek a deeper understanding to be understood. If we do not break down our own motivations from the start, to say that success is not sexually transmitted is a very fair, apparent, and quite obvious statement. As stated before what we value and put out there is the honey we put out to attract those who find what you are putting out there appealing.

When engaging for a look, a status, to fill an empty void. We find we are left still seeking for what we are truly yearning for,

which is a true internal
connection with another,
another who we can share
with and know deeply. But
when we from early on
justify seeking external
modes of attention, status
and appeal we then easily
justify dating, and
marrying for looks, status,
money, and how others will
perceive my 'soul mate' in
comparison to their 'mate'

based on how well they look, the car they drive, the vacations we take and the status I think I give off. On top of that this image feeds into the perception of being somewhat exclusive, so now not only are we feeding into external validation with our spouse, but we are now engaging with others who do the same, therefore justifying this. While all along that innate urge to feel truth, to feel passion with another for internal passions we are still so pulled to.

The idea of continually feeding external validation leading to using that same motive for picking a spouse, is the idea that the image they portray the money they bring the status they hold is now an external object that our external motivation is seeking. Then our spouse becomes a 'success' we have obtained, our spouse becomes our mate who in our own perception feed our external desire to be 'better than', thus; Success is not sexually transmitted.

The perception of success is a win/loose concept rather than a learning/growing one.

The idea of sexually transmitted is the idea that the image this spouse embodies will somehow flow over onto you now being that they are "yours"?

When this is not truly our innate; what we want, who we are, or what we need.

With an externally validated drive we will always be left feeling empty, dry, and searching for another filler. On the other hand growing and internally validated passion and drive will leave us content, inspired and more peaceful.

"It is neither wealth nor splendor; but tranquility and occupation which give you happiness"

-Thomas Jefferson

Chapter 3

Growing an internally inspired passionate partnership, even if already far down the road of living externally validated.

Start small or grandiose, start with what inspires you, meaning wherever your curiosity goes, let it guide you and go with it. If you do not have free time start with one day every other week to take for yourself, and only yourself. If you have a spouse encourage them to do the same. Request to share each others journeys of that day, to share what you did and discovered. And grow this!

If you feel it is positive try something like taking an hour every other day to research your own internal interests and passions. Let it grow in whatever direction your curiosity pulls, and do not be afraid to share this, you will be surprised how quickly you meet others with the same interests, or how many people you already know with those same interests. Let time take.. time, and allow the shift.

"Don't settle for a relationship that won't let you be yourself."

-Oprah Winfrey

Looking for more resources for building a positive foundation checkout:

Amazon life learning books search: Britney Anne Klump
Instagram: _Just.b___
Facebook: @just.b.llc
YouTube: Britney Anne
YouTube: Just.b The Island

Always the very best, with love,

-Britney Anne Klump

Made in the USA
Columbia, SC
05 April 2023

14387031R00022